Entering a Competition

How would you feel if you were in a national competition? Would you be nervous? Would you be excited?

Maya Ying Lin knows how it feels to compete. In 1981, she was a college student studying **architecture**, the art and science of building. She entered a competition to design a **memorial** to honor the men and women who had served in the Vietnam War. The memorial would be built in Washington, D.C.

Maya Lin was only 21 years old when she entered a national design competition.

The Vietnam Veterans Memorial is Maya Lin's most famous work.

Lin's design was simple. The earth was to look as if it had been cut open, representing a wound or a scar. Two black granite walls would rise out of the ground and meet at an angle. They were to look like open arms or an open book. One wall would point to the Washington Monument, and the other would point to the Lincoln Memorial.

The walls would be more than 10 feet high and more than 245 feet long. Each wall would have 70 **panels**, or connected sections.

Names of American soldiers would be placed on the walls. Some of the soldiers died in the Vietnam War, and some were never found. The names would be listed in time order, telling when each soldier died or was declared missing. That way, **veterans** would be able to find their friends.

The largest wall panels would have 137 lines of names. The smallest would have one line. There would be five names, one-half inch tall, on each line. Each name would tell of a person who was loved and missed.

Lin's design won. Some people were not pleased that the design was chosen. Some thought the honor should not go to a person of Chinese **heritage**. They felt that way because China and Vietnam are neighboring countries. China, where Lin's parents came from, also has a **Communist** government, like the one that the United States fought against in the Vietnam War.

Other people thought Lin's design was too plain. Some wanted the names to be in alphabetical order. However, Lin bravely stood by her plan. She wanted the memorial to show the effects of war. She wanted a place where veterans could feel welcome and families and friends could mourn loved ones.

Lin paid close attention to the way the memorial was built. She did not want to disturb the earth more than necessary, and she wanted to save as many trees as possible. She wanted her design to work with the land. Lin said, "The area should be made into a park for all the public to enjoy."

The National Mall, Washington, D.C.

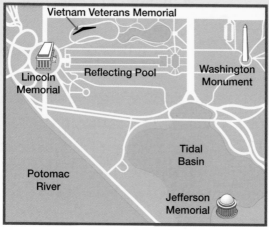

The Vietnam Veterans Memorial was **dedicated** in 1982. It has had more visitors than any other memorial in the country. As people walk toward it, they can see themselves in the shiny surface. It is as if they become a part of the walls.

Lin remembers the first time she visited the new memorial. She found the name of a friend's father on the wall and touched it. "I was reacting to it [the way] I had designed it," she said. Lin's first public work was only the beginning of her career.

Maya Lin was born in 1959 in Athens, Ohio. Her parents had **emigrated** from China to live in the United States. They both taught at Ohio State University. Her father was an artist, and her mother was a poet. Maya loved to read and try new art projects.

Sometimes she played in the hills and woods behind the house she shared with her parents and her brother, Tan. The woods and hills would have a strong effect on her work.

Maya Lin was a top student. Because she loved art and math, she decided to study architecture at Yale University in New Haven, Connecticut. She made the design for the Vietnam Veterans Memorial as an assignment for a class. In 1981, Lin earned a bachelor of arts degree in architecture. She continued to study architecture at Yale and received a master's degree in 1986.

Lin (inset) studied at Yale School of Architecture.

Architecture is thought of as one of the oldest art forms. Architects design buildings, such as houses and schools. They also design furniture, monuments, and parks. Architects think about how things look and go together. They also think about comfort and safety. First, they draw and make models. Then, they work with other people to complete the projects.

Lin does not separate her art from her architecture. "Each of my works originates from a simple desire to make people aware of their surroundings," she has said.

Would you like to be an architect?

First, ask yourself these questions:

- Do I like to look at unusual buildings?
- Do I notice parks and monuments?
- Do I like to learn about people and places?
- Do I like to draw?
- Do I like to make designs on the computer?
- Do I get good grades in math and science?

If you answered "yes" to the above questions, then here is what you can do:

- Study art, history, foreign languages, social studies, science, mechanical drawing, math, and computers in school.
- Earn a college degree in architecture.
- Pass a design test.
- Work as an intern with an architect, engineer, or contractor.
- Take a state-licensing exam on design, construction, materials, and safety.
- Join an architecture firm, or work on your own.

Until Justice Rolls Down

In 1988, Lin was invited to meet with directors of a **civil rights** center about designing a memorial. The civil rights movement involved the actions of many people who wanted to make sure all Americans were treated fairly, no matter what their skin color or beliefs might be. The memorial would honor the workers who were killed because they tried to change unfair laws.

Lin wanted to know more about the workers. She read books and watched films. Then she flew to Montgomery, Alabama, to discuss the project.

On the plane, Lin read a famous speech. It was "I Have a Dream" by Dr. Martin Luther King Jr. One part jumped out at her. It read, "We will not be satisfied until justice rolls down like waters and **righteousness** like a mighty stream."

Suddenly, Lin knew that water must be a part of the Civil Rights Memorial. She made a drawing on a napkin.

Lin was hoping the piece would involve people in different ways. She wanted more than names to be on this memorial. She wanted it to be like a history book. She wanted it to tell a story, showing how events caused people's deaths and the deaths caused events to happen.

Lin saw a place where the memorial could go. The area would need to be changed so that it would fit, but the center's directors liked Lin's ideas. They agreed to make the changes to the area. They also gave her a list of important events to show with the names.

Lin designed a round, black granite table. A time line was carved onto the top. Water came from the center of the table and flowed over the edge. It was as if history was bubbling up from the earth. The words that had inspired Lin were on the wall behind the table. Water flowed over the wall, too.

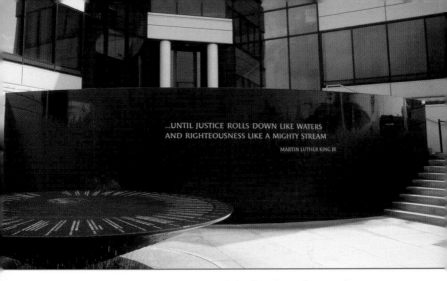

The Civil Rights Memorial is a part of the Southern Poverty Law Center in Montgomery, Alabama.

The Civil Rights Memorial was dedicated in 1989. Just as Lin planned, people can experience the memorial in several ways. They can touch and hear the water, read the words, and think about the events and the many people who died.

The memorial honors the past, but it is also for the future. Lin wants each visitor to the memorial to learn from the work of those who died. The time line has been left open to show that we must never stop working for the civil rights of all people.

Sculptures

Lin used water again for a project she designed for Yale University. It was a sculpture, not a memorial.

A sculpture is a kind of **three-dimensional** art form. It can be made from almost anything. **Sculptors** use stone, metal, clay, or wood. Some use paper, ivory, or wax. Others use soap, plastic, trash, or even the earth.

Sculptures can show any kind of subject. They can also be formed in different ways. They can be carved, which means that parts are cut away until the right shape is reached. They can also be modeled, meaning that parts are built up to make the shape. Sculptures can also be cast, or formed in a mold, or made of parts put together.

The sculpture that Yale asked Lin to create was dedicated in 1993. It tells the story of the women students at Yale through the years.

Yale University

Many schools today accept both male and female students, although some schools have only one or the other. However, when Yale University opened in the eighteenth century, only men could **enroll**.

That didn't change until 1873, when 13 women enrolled. Now, thousands of women go to Yale.

Lin had to think about what she wanted her sculpture to say. First, she found out that women had been students at Yale all along.

Women's Table is in front of the Sterling Memorial Library at Yale University.

However, there were no records of the women because they were not allowed to enroll. They were only able to visit some classes as long as they were silent. "I wanted to make them seen and heard," Lin said.

Lin created another water table. This one was made of green granite. She decided to use a **spiral** pattern on top that had a beginning but no end. At first, she wanted words to be part of the pattern.

Lin changed her mind. Instead of words, she used numbers. The table has a winding spiral of numbers, starting with zero and ending with the number 4,823. These numbers showed how many women had enrolled at Yale through the years.

The sculpture is called *Women's Table*. The end of the spiral is open. Why might she have done that?

Another of Lin's outdoor sculptures is called *Wave Field*. Completed in 1995, it shows her deep interest in nature.

Wave Field is made of a combination of soil and sand to keep its shape.

The sculpture is at the University of Michigan in Ann Arbor. A piece of earth, 100 by 100 feet, is shaped with 50 grass waves in 8 rows. To some it looks like the sea, to some a desert, and to others a wheat field. Lin wants people to relax, study, and play there.

The Motion Picture Industry honored Lin in 1995. Have you heard of the Academy Awards®? In 1995, a film about Lin won this award for Best **Documentary**. The film is called *Maya Lin: A Strong Clear Vision*. It tells about the Vietnam Veterans Memorial. It also tells about Lin's other work. The film shows how she starts with an idea about how she wants to make people feel. Then she turns the idea into something real.

Maya Lin has continued to work as an architect as well as a sculptor. She never wanted to choose between the two fields.

One of Lin's buildings is the Langston Hughes Library. The library is named for a famous writer. Completed in 1999, the building is on a farm near Clinton, Tennessee. Maya used a barn that was built in the 1860s to build the library. Its purpose is to hold research materials about civil rights.

The Langston Hughes Library in Tennessee is in a former barn.

19

Lin's list of projects keeps growing. These projects have included some unusual clocks and a park with a skating rink. Tiny lights in a rink form a pattern that looks like stars. How does she get all of her great ideas?

First of all, Lin studies. She reads about the past and about people all around the world. She also reads a lot about science. In addition, Lin tries to understand the work of other artists.

Another way Lin gets her ideas is by looking to the environment. She uses the colors and shapes that she sees. She uses light and darkness. Lin looks for ways to recycle. Materials found in nature are often used in her work.

Lin uses many art forms and a lot of different materials. She might begin with a pencil drawing, or she might make a design using a computer.

Lin always finishes her work in the same way. She likes to name it. "I see the name as its final shape," she has said, "and once it has its name, it's on its own."

Maya Lin has won many awards for her work. Many people ask her to make speeches about her work, but she is so busy that she must often say no. However, she serves on the boards of many **civic** groups. Lin enjoys helping people and the environment.

Lin wanted a way to better explain her work, so she wrote a book called *Boundaries*. It was published in 2000. "This book gives a sense of my projects and the process I go through to make them," she said.

Lin lives in New York City with her husband and two daughters. She works at her studio there. Lin is proud of her work, but she is humble, too. "I do not believe anything I can create can compare to the beauty of the natural world," she said, "but these works are a response to that beauty."

Vietnam Veterans Memorial (1982)

Location: Washington, D.C.
Art Form: Memorial
Description: V-shaped black granite
walls engraved with more than
58,000 names

Civil Rights Memorial (1989)

Location: Montgomery, Alabama
Art Form: Memorial
Description: Circular black
granite table with flowing water

Topo (1991)

Location: Sports Coliseum in Charlotte, North Carolina
Art Form: Earthwork sculpture **topiary**
Description: Bushes shaped like large balls rolling down a hill
toward a "hole in one"

Women's Table (1993)

Location: Yale University, New Haven, Connecticut
Art Form: Sculpture
Description: Water table made
of green granite with a spiral of numbers on top

The Museum for African Art (1993)

Location: New York City
Art Form: Building loft
Description: A large room for displaying arts and crafts; symbolizes a journey from night into day

Groundswell (1993)

Location: Ohio State University, Columbus, Ohio
Art Form: Sculpture
Description: Curves created from 43 tons of clear and dark green broken glass

Eclipsed Time (1995)

Location: Penn Station, New York City
Art Form: Sculpture
Description: 38-foot elliptical hanging clock

Norton Residence (1998)

Location: New York City
Art Form: Building
Description: A home with parts that can "fold up" to change its shape

Glossary

architecture the art and science of building

civic relating to a city and its people

civil rights a guarantee of citizens' personal liberty

Communist a system of government that emphasizes the needs of the state rather than individual freedoms

dedicated opened to public use

documentary a film that presents factual information

emigrated left one country intending to live in another

enroll to become a member

heritage background or traditions

memorial a monument or anything that helps people remember a person or event

panels flat sections that are part of a surface

righteousness fairness

sculptors artists who produce works of sculpture

spiral a winding shape

three-dimensional having height, width, and depth

topiary art made from trimming shrubs or trees into unusual shapes

veterans people who have served in the armed forces